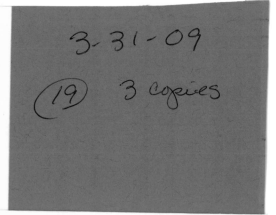

3-31-09

(19)   3 copies

3/02

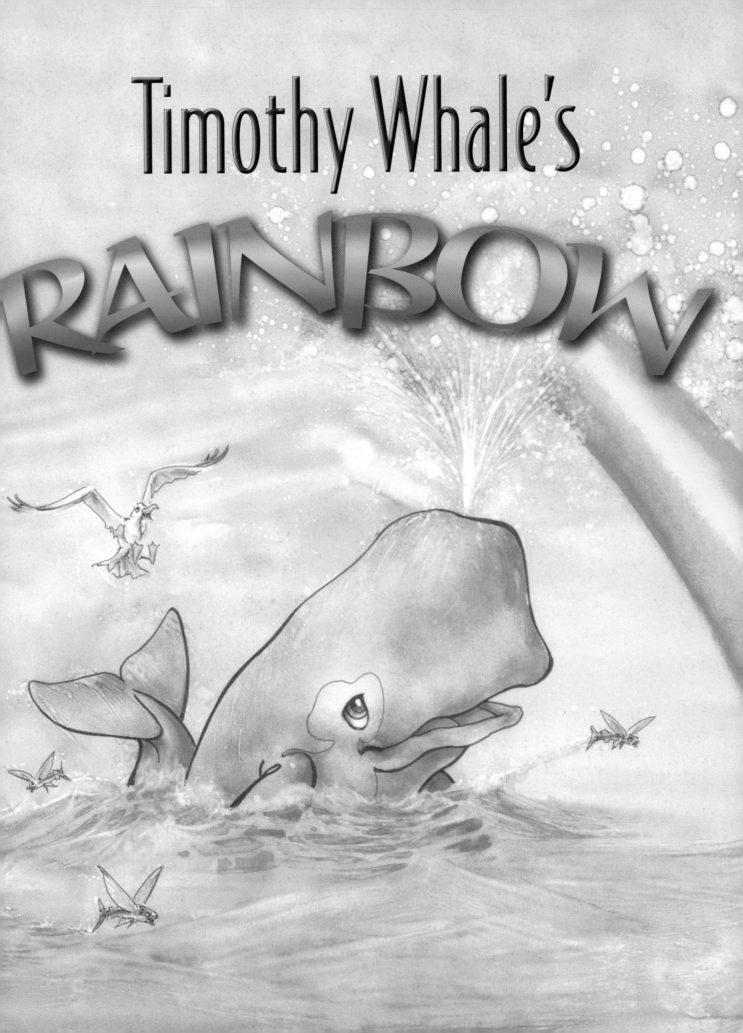

Timothy Whale's
RAINBOW

Dedicated to

our grand kids

and their parents

Timothy Whale's RAINBOW

Darrell Wiskur

MB
Master
Books

First Printing: October 2000

Please visit our website for other great titles: www.masterbooks.net

ISBN: 0-89051-289-2
Library of Congress: 00-102647

Printed in the United States of America.

*T*imothy Whale is who I am
The largest mammal known to man.

1 grow in length to sixty feet ~

*M*y spout is seen by many a fleet.

On bright sunny days, aye, 'tis something to see
I blow me spout, as high as can be.

Then right before me very eyes
Beautiful colors appear in the sky.

Mates, it set me to wondering how this could be,
So I asked my grandfather – he's wiser than me.
And what he told me 'tis really true
Come on along, and I'll tell it to you.

We must go back to Noah's time . . .

*T*was nary a ship of any kind.

An ark was the craft God told Noah to build; with two of each animal let it be filled.

Mocking God and calling Noah insane, People in that day knew nothing of rain.

*I*nto the ark creatures came two by two

People just laughed and called it a zoo.

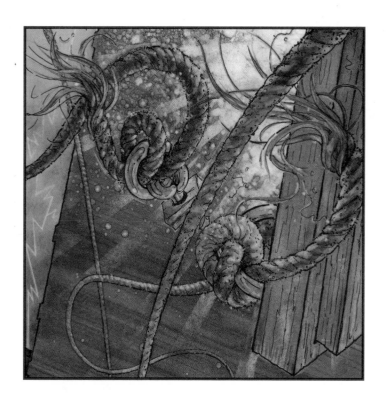

W ith all safe inside,
God shut the door.
People didn't know they would
see Noah no more. All of a
sudden the sky gave a roar. Out
of the heavens, the water just
poured. Fountains of water sprang
forth on dry land. For all wicked
people the end was at hand.

*D*on't feel bad – they chose their lot

Aye, with wicked hearts Noah's God they mocked.

orty days, forty nights, it rained and rained

*T*he earth was covered —
all life was claimed.

To search new earth
Noah sent a raven
Next a dove to find safe haven.

*A*ll seeds replanted by churning seas
Replenished the earth with
plants, flowers, and trees.

*T*was her third flight out,
that the dove found a home.
She was free ~ but still all alone.

When God commanded
all left the ark
To a fresh cleaned earth
and a grand new start.

Noah and his
family, whose
lives were spared,
To the God of Heaven
an altar prepared.

God blessed Noah
and gave him a sign
Aye, one that would
last 'til the end of time.

Noah was first to
see God's sign –
A beautiful rainbow
from a cloud did shine.

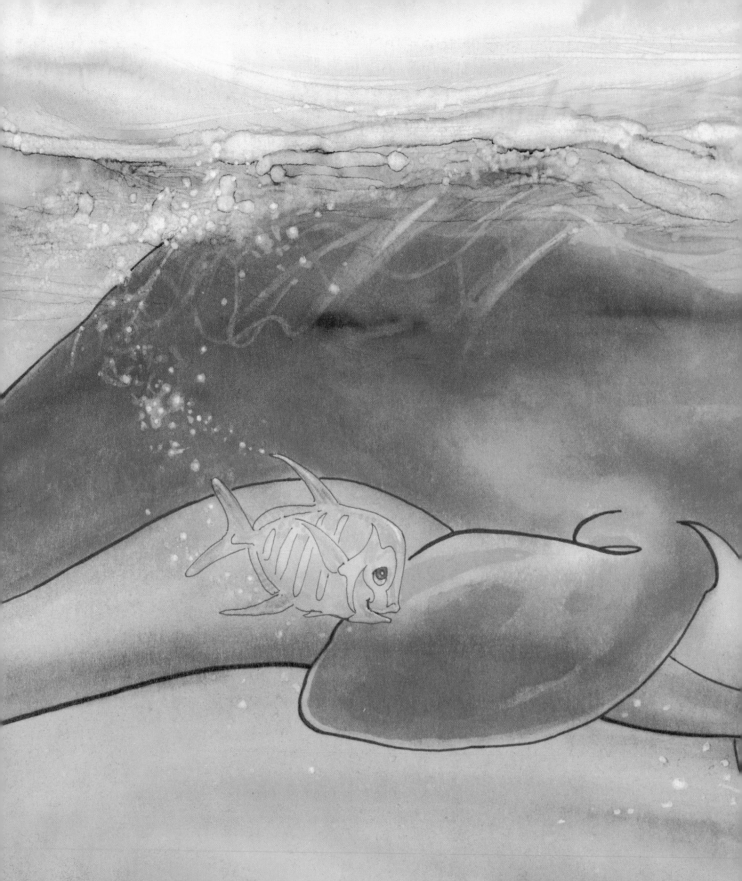

So there you have it, plain as can be,

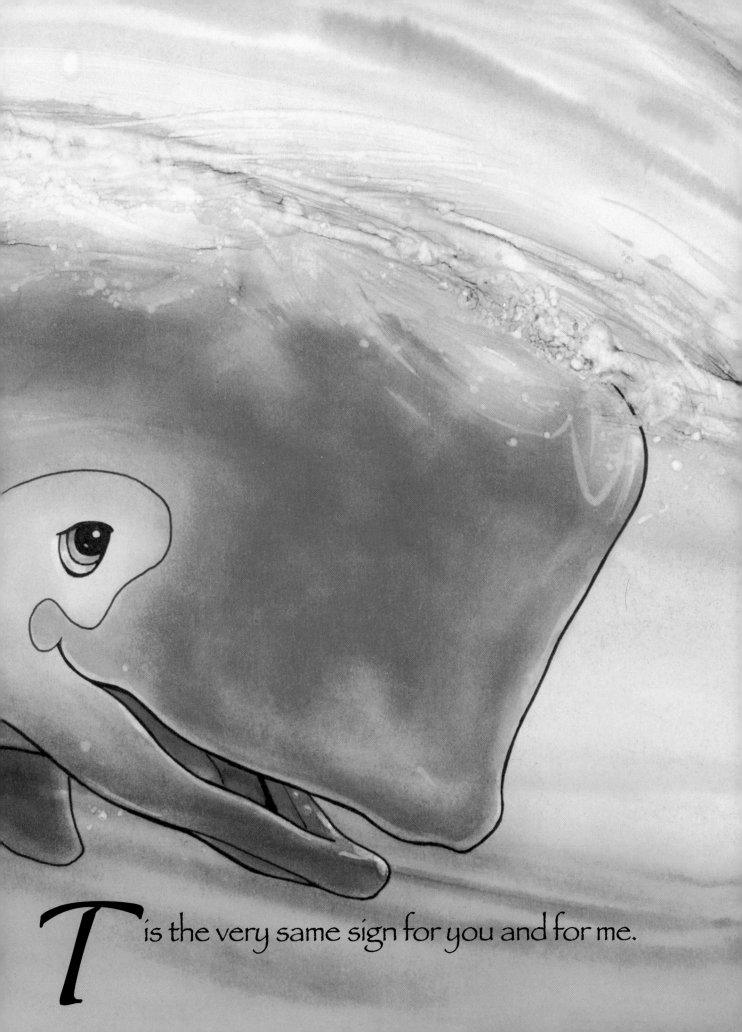

T is the very same sign for you and for me.

1 give up me spray, we look through the mist,

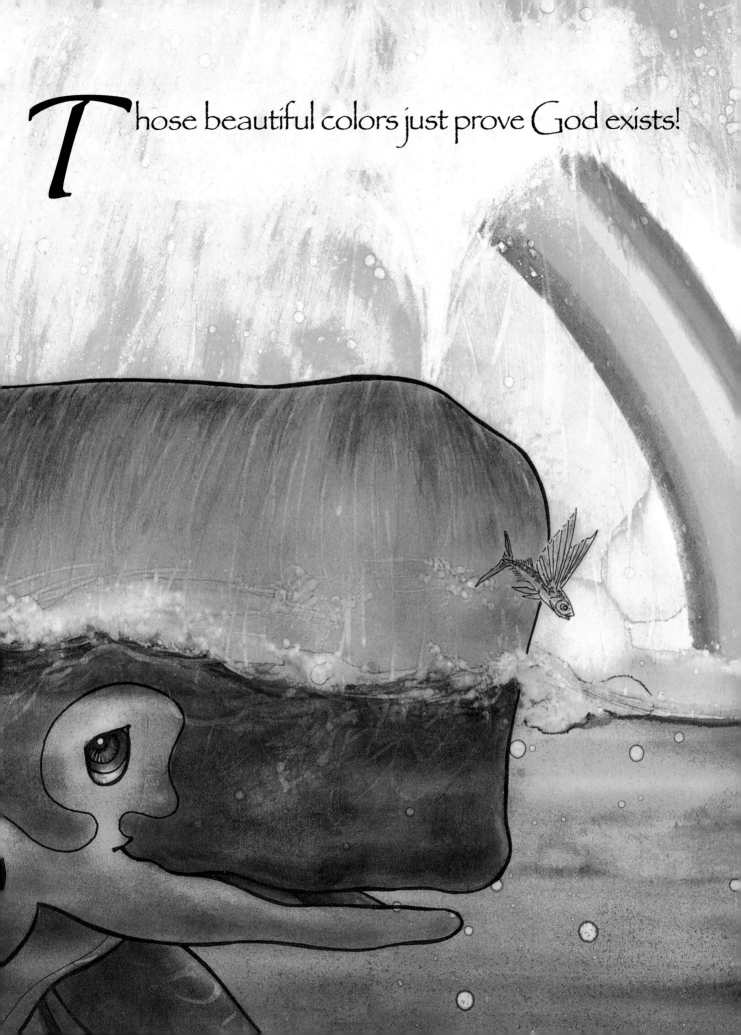

*T*hose beautiful colors just prove God exists!

Whale Notes
(cetaceans)

The character in this book, Timothy Whale, is a sperm whale.

Whales are the largest creatures ever created, bigger by tons than the biggest dinosaurs.

For classification, whales, dolphins and porpoises are of the order Cetacea.

There are two surviving sub-orders of whales: toothed whales, of which there are 67 species, and baleen whales, of which there are 11 species.

Baleen whales do not have teeth for feeding; instead they have plates of baleen that hang from their upper jaw as filters to strain food from the water.

Whales are warm-blooded mammals—not fish—and need air to live.

The head of the sperm whale is one-third its body length and it has the largest, most complex brain of any animal on earth. This amazing creature is able to remain submerged for over two hours and forage at depths of over 3,000 feet.

Blue Whale: up to 110 feet, 150 tons

Bowhead Whale: up to 50 feet, 60 tons

Beards Whale: up to 50 feet, 20 tons

Sei Whale: up to 60 feet, 25 tons

Fin Whale: up to 88 feet, 80 tons

Humpback Whale: up to 60 feet, 60 tons

Right Whale: up to 55 feet, 40 tons

Sperm Whale: up to 60 feet, 50 tons

Glossary Notes and Biblical Commentary

Rainbows

Rainbows are formed when sunlight strikes drops of water falling from a rain cloud. The droplets scatter the light into its spectrum, the different colors that reach our eyes.

Altar

A raised platform: the place where sacrifices and offerings were made to God. In giving thanks for a new beginning, ". . . Noah built an altar unto the Lord; and took of every clean beast and of every clean fowl, and offered burnt offerings on the altar" (Genesis 8:20).

Sign

A mark or symbol that has a specific meaning: ' set my bow in the clouds, and it shall be for a sig of a covenant between me and the earth (Genesis 9:13). The rainbow is th sign of God's covenant to ma that He would never destro the earth again by wate (Genesis 9:11-17

Whale Spout

Whales must come to the surface in order to breathe air. Upon reaching the surface, the whale exhales the air (not water) from its lungs. This warm air condenses when it contacts the cold sea air creating water vapor and the "spout" associated with whales.

Ark

God gave Noah instructions for building an ark that would have perfect dimensions for a stable ride in the turbulent flood waters and high seas for months with its precious live cargo safe and dry inside.

The ark was 450 feet long, 75 feet wide and 45 feet high, with three stories.

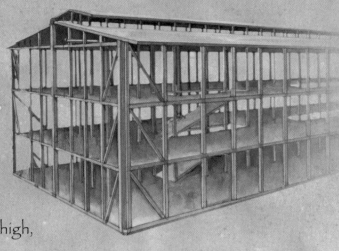

Seed for Life

A dried part from a flowering plant that typically contains the embryo with its protective coat and stored food that will develop into a new plant anytime it is planted in an environment that nourishes the seed to sprout. It might lay dormant or "dead" looking as a dried seed for a long time.

Two by Two

Creatures went into the ark by twos, the male and his female, except for the clean beasts (Genesis 7:2). Noah took by sevens the clean beasts, the male and female, because they were selected by God for sacrifice and food. After the flood, the clean beasts were domesticated for Noah's new work of animal husbandry.

Family

After leaving the ark, the male and female of each kind of animal became the father and mother of a new family that would fill the earth with many more animals.

Biography

Darrell Wiskur has worked as an illustrator and product designer for 35 years. "*Timothy Whale's Rainbow*" is his first book for Master Books.

Darrell lives with his wife, Pat, in a cozy home near a beautiful lake in the Ozark Mountains of Arkansas.

He studied at the Chicago Art Institute, the Chicago Academy of Fine Art and the Bill Baker School of Design. He has illustrated more than 50 titles in the areas of wildlife and children's literature.